AF267619

Wanderer and the Moon

Andreana Warlow

a poetry and prose collection

Independently published 2021
ISBN: 978-1-7776740-0-7

To My Wondrous Mother,

you are the strength running through my veins and the light shining through my dark. I am forever grateful for your unwavering support, guidance—everything you've ever given me.

"We delight in the beauty of the butterfly, but rarely admit the changes it has gone through to achieve that beauty."

- Maya Angelou

Contents

I. Waning Moon: on love

II. New Moon: on sorrow

III. Full Moon: on growth

I.

Waning Moon

on love

PREFACE

Through late-night reflections, my words
come together to create art—flowing
steadily, freely, muddled or blurred.
It's when I should be sleeping that they mingle
to make the most sense—combined, designed
in this crowded head of mine.
All the could've been-should've been's, and still
needing to say, mixed with stories for others
who also need comfort on their way.
Weaving tales from experiences gone and
varying perspectives.

I create to embrace all I can't be near in hopes
my words land in the hearts of people—familiar and
those I've yet to meet, as our lines have crossed in the plans.
The restless wanderer's musings illuminated
by the healing moon. The free-spirited archer
—wanting nothing more than to live in her truth,
wanting the same for you.

LIFTED

Hold me under the light of the moon,
so few stars in sight.
The sounds of day have drifted away,
gone with the beaming bright.
Follow me into the nether
as we head to cloud nine.
Our bodies tangled together with
your heart bound to mine.

A PENNY FOR YOUR THOUGHTS

5

One place I always dreamt of going
is where the wild things are.
Perhaps I would find some peculiar
new friends to adore. It's not only
that I wander off to places I've never seen.
But when they're talking, I realize
I've wandered into the heads
of strangers trying to decipher their wildest dreams.
Imagining being in their mind's eye,
picking apart the ins and outs of all that
makes them who they are.
Trying on their shoe's, guessing what
it might take for us to match in size.

I'm thinking of you and why
you do the things you do.
What are the details in the fabric you bite
your tongue to remain unsaid?
Maybe one day we can talk about this
together, face to face.

SOUL-MATES

For what was just a blip
in time, an instant—you
completed me, despite me.
Thank you for teaching, guiding,
inspiring, and loving me.
Thank you for being you.
You'll always be with me,
undeniably.

MUSINGS

It's the simplest things in life we overlook and take for granted. Chirps at sunrise before the snow has cleared. Morning dew on a new summer day. Cheerful greetings on an afternoon stroll. Having loved ones draw you near and embrace you for who you are.

HOPE SPRINGS ETERNAL

8

Cherished moments between meeting
and leaving; warm embraces,
a shelter from life's storms, shoulders
to lean on and, romance in the dullest places.
Once upon a time—keep the history of
love gone framed in your mind.
These memories provide hope
where happiness can spring again.
Joy and blessings hidden in
heartbreak lessons.

SHADES OF GREEN

I took a chance reading all the faves,
books leaving everyone in a rave.
The one I have been waiting for
has yet to be made; with all my appetite saved up,
it is a special one I crave.
Or the first and its sequel.
Or a trilogy set.
No mention of how many there would be
those years ago that you said to me:

Another one of your creations is to be a
book about your life, the story of who
and the world before you.
All that you sacrificed to travel from there and
why you needed to be here.

Perhaps this is what's drawn me to writing.
I'm pulling out words buried deep down inside
from a range of experiences and emotions
I desperately tried to hide.
You know as well as I;
parts of our lives can only stay
buried in the sand for so long,
until the beach gets flooded by the tide.
I drifted out in the ocean
drowning in my tears and hoping:

One day you'll enjoy reading
this collection of work I've passed the time creating.
Thousands of words written

in these months we've been waiting.
Waiting for your well-needed rest
and well-deserved healing.
And soon we will all be together again
—it's only a matter of time.

ALTERNATIVELY, BLACK PEPPER

Of all the things
this world has
to offer.

Cinnamon

I don't know why
but it always has
me thinking of you.

It must have been one of your
favorites, too.

ACROSS OCEANS

I see you though I may never
reach where you are.
I hear you when I read between
the lines of your deepest thoughts.
If all that's to be are pictures
and words from your soul,
then wrap them with a ribbon
—your presence in presents to behold.

CRYSTAL BALL

I exist between
here,
there,
everywhere.
Far away and back again.
I am floating up above
and hovering down below.
Self-reliant, independent
to a fault.
It feels as if a few self-inflicted
wounds are unresolved.
Under the surface, hidden from sight
with you stuck on my mind.
I used to desire living life alone,
now I can't get over the idea of
you in my life.
At a distance, at an arm's length,
where our eyes can meet
only for a glance.
Mouths shut,
speaking only through telepathy.
Because our souls
are connected
even when our hands
are disconnected.

ACROBATS

14

Frozen in time,
suspended in air.
Let's stay together,
be forever there.

BUT A DREAM

In a realm of cotton candy dreams,
the autumn breeze blows
and whispers gentle melodies.
Visions from the past,
I recognize the voice of you.
On these hills I've found, I lay to rest
my worries; and forgive myself for the days
spent in a flurry. In a rush to discover the world
with inabilities to love without hindrance.
Nature speaks to me as I stand with the
mystic winds and remember the times I had you
beside me, here. It is in the way the fragrant flowers grow,
and the seasons' colours begin to show
that I feel your love and sense you nearby.

AN ODE TO A STAR

Oh, how I love the sight of you,
such mastery in the way you move.
How you fill up my morning cup
and make my arms stretch to the ceiling.
Your ability to reach every crevasse,
enhancing life with even the shortest rays.
To go days without you shining,
I'm as gloomy as the clouds, grey,
and doing all to pass the time
until your uplifting light beams down again.

NATURE FEELS

Your name I've been craving;
smooth and sweet, delectably,
flowing off the tip of my tongue.
As if poured from my ambrosial mouth
repeatedly before this all-day marathon began.
Sheer fluidity of our bodies combined,
reminiscent of the celestial place
we've visited in previous lifetimes.
Midnight moans and intoxicating whispers
from love's dictionary are the sweetest verses.
We're heating up and coming together slowly,
like honey flowing in a hurry.

SHINE BRIGHT

18

So many stars
flickering, blinding
as we get lost
in each other tonight.

MENTAL SCREEN-SHOT

19

That is when I saw you shining like
I never had before. A moment
to be captured, placed in a locket.
Held close to my heart—forever.
Because time is always fleeting, I may never
get this chance again to see you glow
so brightly and feel this happy.

HOPE-FULL

Wrapped up in my love, I'll always
hold you close. Gazing into gentle, sweet eyes
and feeling your fresh soft skin, I discovered
the unlimited amount of love and affection
I had to give and to receive.
Inside of me, you grew—the first home
in this life you knew. I finally understand
Motherhood is a gift, an incredible role
I had to grow in, too.

ON THE WEEKND

Wearing fluorescent yellow with a laugh
that bellowed. The very sight of him set
my soul on fire and the bass in his voice
enhanced my desires. Aching legs too tired
after work to journey home that day.
Sore feet with the only sense to
guide me home another way.

To the big box store that serves our
wants and needs. In earshot of a man
hollering on the phone who almost
brought me to my knees.
In awe, of course, after I turned and glanced.
Amazed! Eyes stuck, star-struck!
Can you imagine if I had dilly-dallied?
Would we have missed our chance?

I must've turned bright red, blushing
with no hiding my smile. It was such
a long day at work even so, all I wanted
was to stay, spend time and chat for a while.
He could've told me a long story about
an old lady who lived in a shoe.
Or about whales I'd never heard of.
I would've nodded and pretended
I knew about them too.

ROCK THE BOAT

22

Your existence became an anchor in this life of turbulence.

EUPHORIA

The gift of gab, your undisputed way
with words; majestically stringing them together,
pulsating deep in my soul as you speak.
Hungrily, I consume your creations,
am blinded by temptations,
transported to otherworldly destinations.
I become a feather for your hands alone;
hold me as carefully or roughly as you please.
Dip me in your pot of ink—we'll
compose endless love stories.

RITUALS AND TRADITIONS

It feels like it's been ages since
we were able to be together for a day.
Out of our busy schedules,
meeting mid-town to spend some time
and chat about all the things we have to say.
A chance to be mellow, enjoy a meal and
hang out for a while, just you and I.
Then walk through the towers with
busy people bustling by.

Browse through thousands
of books upon the shelves.
Discuss over the music playing
titles we'd like to check out,
split up and wander by ourselves.
Order a coffee or tea and, of course,
speak about things some more.
This ritual tried and true,
a go-to for years now.
All the talking made up for years
of words left unsaid by us two.
Conversations I'd have with myself of
things I'd hope to talk about one day,
me and you.

Because we were together every day
until the day we were not.
The 'us' became a void, and the distance felt
too far from your arms to my heart.
So, I'm happy and grateful for all the days
space between us ceases to remain.

The moments I get to see your face
and we have conversations that
with others don't flow the same.
We're able to be together for a while
and talk of all the things so
shocking, peculiar,
random, and
mundane.

HEAVEN ON EARTH

Looking at the twinkling lights,
I always think of you.
Bright-eyed with a big heart,
and a smile to warm your soul.

I miss you most at Christmas time.

MAYBE

27

Can you imagine staying
this way forever.
Stillness and the warmth
of love, lust,
desire, and bliss.
Meticulous moments in time
led up to this.

RED LIGHT SPECIAL

Blurry eyes, tunnel vision,
touching each other with such ease.
Both hearts racing,
blood rushing at the speed of light.
There's no place in existence I'd rather be.
When we're too far apart,
I'm lusting for you in every single way.
Especially when memories replay
of you moaning my name—so perfectly.

A VISION

29

Everything I imagined you to be, and more.
The rose that grew from concrete,
undeniable strength and beauty to adore.

SHADOW REALM

It won't always be rainbows and
butterflies but we can make it through
the hard times. From the shadows, we take
turns to pull each other out. To your arms I
know to which I can always run.

TEASE

Strip first, let us get down to the
naked truth as we converse.
Put it all on the table, bare your soul.
I want to know about what life has
blessed you, everything that's cursed.
Tell me your secrets while staring into my eyes.
Please, don't disguise your true desires
while in my life. Take my hand and lead me
to a garden where our love sets the mood.
We'll fade the lines between tantalizing and
subdued. Foreign lovers romancing will
only work by starting with both slates clean;
intentions revealed, no hidden motives behind
the scene. So, strip first, we'll get down
to the naked truth before our bodies can converse.

DOUBLE INFINITY

32

On bended knee,
your hand in mine.
Forever yours
until the end of time.

LIGHT AS A FEATHER

Feeling free, you have given me space
to grow into a person I am proud to be.
Proud to be known, proud to be loved
—loved by you in all the ways
I never imagined for me.

CHESHIRE CAT

34

Of life's simple pleasures, your smile tops my list.

LITTLE GENIUSES

35

Listen to the children,
they'll tell all that's important.
About the games to be played
and quality time to spend.
It's not just about the material
but joys to be shared.

VIBE

It comes along one day
falling out of the sky.
That stirring you feel inside
just looking in their eyes.

A TALE OF DESIRE

37

Shadows dancing in a room dim-lit red
to the rhythm of fading heartbeats.
An alluring tone set for two to sway
as one leads the way.
Long-awaited caresses, no more delaying,
they've finally found where bliss is.
Twin flames eternally burning
bright. Tethered souls entangled in bed,
phantoms of the night.

JUST SO

Your mouth speaks the only language my body understands and craves.

COMPASS

39

My north star,
the guide to all I know.
I'll always journey back to you,
within you I've found a home.

BUILT TO LAST

40

Standing firm, holding tight
through rip tides and hurricanes
—my love for you as strong as
our early days.

STARGAZING

41

Have you ever sat staring and realized just how captivated you were? Stuck in a trance with time fleeting, wondering why an entity this beautiful and precious was gifted to bless your presence.

TWENTY-TWENTY VISION

42

Forget Me Nots and Tiger-Lilies;
Roses, Sunflowers, and more.
It wasn't until the world was grey
that I noticed all the beauty to adore.
Overwhelmed in isolation,
counting down the days.
Until masks become a thing of the past
and the world becomes bright again.

SAVING GRACE

43

We'll bend, we'll fold
but break we will not.
Wake up with a new slate
as we start each day.
Together is where
I put my faith.

SO, THIS IS CHRISTMAS

In the years growing up, our home
never had a Christmas tree, the holiday felt bare.
I remember you'd say you didn't like the décor,
but I think it was because there was no money there.
It's all the more heartbreaking now as our house is
ornament dressed but instead of
season's greetings, hugs, and cheer—we
can't even be near.

I wish I could buy you a bottle of perfume
or a pair of fluffy plush slippers. Have the kids
draw a picture to mail, even make you dinner.
During all my years, this Christmas will be
the strangest of them all. We'll only be allowed
to visit on a video call.

You'll see us, and we'll see you.
Mentally you're trying your hardest
to respond, though you're unable to.
So, until I can listen to your voice again or
you're alert for video chats,
I replay our last conversation in my mind
when you said, "I love you all" and
"we'll talk tomorrow".

And hopefully, my wishes for you will
come true this supposed most joyous
season of them all.

PITCH-BLACK

45

Always in the dawn
when it's calmest,
do I hear your voice
calling my name.

PLAYING FOR KEEPS

Too many rounds to count
your body spent with mine.
All the days, all the ways
we occupied our time.
Mountains we climbed, ships
that we sailed. The stories these
walls could tell and secrets our
sheets keep sealed. It's hard to
believe there's skin still untouched
for your hands to sweep. Tally
up the score, seal it with a kiss.
This territory is for you alone,
take your time and savor all of this.

SEALED WITH A KISS

47

I know you felt it as I did
when our fingers intertwined.
Pure, undeniable chemistry each time
your gaze would align with mine.

ONE ON ONE

48

Can we talk freely and revel in a real connection? No crutches to avoid glances. Sit comfortably in the silence. Can we be together without the distractions?

SHOW AND TELL

49

Show me what your love is like,
I'll tell you the way mine goes.
We can agree to disagree
because what comes natural to you
won't feel right to me.

STAY

Always with the lights on, because the darkness buried deep within will swallow us whole before we have a chance to figure out our destined roles. Let's stay tucked away awhile, get lost in all-consuming desires that have burned in our hearts since the first time your glossy eyes locked with mine. Blue is the warmest colour, forever reminding me of you and the hurtful things past trauma forced our hands to do. Unable to see in the dark, I blamed you, unaware of the saving desperately needed within me, too. When the heartache is over, and the Light illuminates through our ghosts that linger in this place, I'll stay a little longer, sitting with love-filled memories that remain.

II.

New Moon
on sorrow

I SPY

53

That is where you'll find me.
Hidden,
out of reach.
Counting my woes,
wallowing too
—on the dark side of the moon.

UP A LITTLE HIGHER

Put your pain upon a pedestal
yearning for relief.
Desperate for an ear to bend,
you've run out of your beliefs.

Heartbroken by responses
from those that claim to love you.
They lead with "how could you reveal that?"
sadder still, think not much of you.

A simple "what happened?' would suffice,
yet now it's you who paid the price.
Feeling too damaged to be cared for,
overly exposed to feel whole.
Put your pieces back together,
lonesome on your pedestal.

TREAD LIGHTLY

55

If not for holding on tight
to threads of sanity, I'd
be completely undone,
unraveling.

SEASONAL DEPRESSION

The strange things I remember,
like that ice-cold day in December.
Walking hand in hand, side by side,
the closest soul I knew whom I could confide in.
Heartbreakingly, after many
trials and tribulations, I failed to give you
my dedication. So, upon inhaling winter air
while being bit by the cold,
my mind flashes back to memories
it beholds. Times I repented my sins and
was unable to correct the wrongs,
as many faults in our stars reflected
parts of us that didn't belong.

One thing I often wonder—do
you ever ponder? Do you ever think back
to those nights in October?
Those mornings in September?
What about meeting in the Spring
when we first began as a fling?
Up late in the summer to stargaze.
The moon and your eyes left me in a daze.
Think of me dearly as the snow falls
and forget me when your new love calls.

SLAPPY

57

Of all the dolls on the shelf,
only one remained.
Untouched, unloved.
Did it even have a name?
There it sat, day after day.
Caked with dust,
desperately in need of play.
Out of reach,
running out of time.
All dolls need love and care
—what about mine?

KEEP YOU RIGHT HERE

What a scene
to end that chapter in our lives.
Two feet out the door,
a stubborn head held high.
Making the grandest exit
of all your withdrawals.
After smashing down my walls
and breaking through my heart.
Though you're physically gone,
will your ghost ever depart?

RALPH'S DAY OUT

An elephant sat on my chest today.
Its soul-crushing weight left me in despair.
Waving my hands up high while
letting out a painful cry.
My sanity disappeared, as did my cares.

Even before it entered the room:
down the hall, out the door
were the footsteps, ground shaking
echoes of doom. It traveled round
hills and yonder to find me in my place
of comfort. A tranquil paradise, peaceful.
It stormed in thundering, reducing
my surrounding walls to rubble.

As it shook my waning core,
I knew I was out of options.
Fight or flight was out the door; this
situation all too familiar, caught in
this predicament before.
Each time the restlessness and irritability set in.
Leaving me sweaty and trembling,
a distraught mess on the floor.

An elephant sat on my chest today and
it is only a matter of time until
Ralph comes back to play.

UNTETHERED

Look at us now, so warped and disconnected.
Our circumstances could be different
if you saw from my perspective.
Had you considered my
pains, fears, and needs,
unwavering hope and respect
could be there in which for us to believe.

Is all fair in love?
Why does it feel like we are at war?

TORRENTIAL RAINS IN MAY

Have you ever sat with heartbreak many moons overdue? Felt your heart aching beyond comprehension while reliving past experiences, remembering life spent and with who. Imagining where you'd be today had you said: "b" instead of "a" or gone left instead of right. Understanding that—that was then and this, this is now. This moment in time and you, set by Destiny to greet.

Have you ever sat with heartbreak many moons overdue? Knowing what you know now, not what you bet you did. You are still revising the script in your mind, having conversations replay that should've went a different way. Wracked with the courage to finally say all you wanted but couldn't at the time. Only you'll ever know there are bits of your existence wishing to go back to before the present became the past. To when you thought you knew it all, thinking there would be nothing to miss. Or realizing you made the wrong decision. Only you will feel the confusion as it washes over your thoughts: catching you off guard, clouding your judgment with imagination and desire—no room left for reality. All the while tempting fate to change the course set.

Have you ever sat with heartbreak many moons overdue? What's paramount is true. Memories are surging through me, memories of you.

GOING UNDER

62

Don't watch me while
I fall from grace,
all my faults exposed.
Just let me lay
in the bed I've made,
set fire to my soul.

LOVE NOTES

Four on the floor
sliding notes under the door.
Asking simple questions,
needing the answers more and more.
Circle yes,
please never no.
Do you love me, do you care?
I wish I could be near.
Waiting on the other side
became a desperate past time,
a solo game left to play.
Always hoping for the day
I could feel the love
this bond is supposed to hold.

KNOW IT ALL

64

I wonder most on days like this, does Destiny have our lives planned out for us? Or has She made this all up along the way as I have? I've been sulking around with my head in my hands, calculating ways to right all these wrongs. Searching for clues to know I'm not wasting my time, because She told me—She, told me, what is for me will be. But She hasn't said why you and I are no longer we.

LIFE LESSONS

65

It's a different kind of heartache to mourn someone while they're still alive.

BURNED WITH DESIRE

After 'The Lesson of the Moth' by Don Marquis

Little creatures fluttering
through the night sky; possessed,
naturally obsessed with moonlight.
Mesmerized and entranced,
circling closer to their prize.
Ultimately landing on the bulb
that'll burn em crisp.
Ill-fated demise.

it happens to us all at some point

WHEN THE BOUGH BROKE

Right from the start, I followed my heart
and pushed for my absolute best.
No matter how difficult the emotions became
to digest. Until eventually drifting farther
into a vast blue ocean on the verge of choking,
I was hoping for an extra hand to hold.
Ready to tap out because it took every fibre
inside of me to find full breaths to make.
The show must go on, so every time I woke,
I'd continue putting my limits to the test.
There was no other choice but to keep
striving, keep surviving.

After the passing of busy hazy days,
I realized I felt lighter and full of joy again
as I just had to depend on my wits,
on my strengths—hold tight to my faith
as it's all completely worth it in the end.
They were growing, changing, these
beautiful beings I created. Although barely,
just barely, I made it. A journey through
glorious hills and strenuous valleys—now
halted at a crossroads, the earth-shattering
fork in my road. There was almost another
who would've been breathtakingly wholesome
like the others.

The role I grew into became challenged, jolted
at the edge. I felt it deep in my soul and
still, entirely do, that another round
would have been too torturous

to make it through.
No more ocean to wade in; I made it
after reaching the brink but would not
have that luck again.

It was the hardest decision I have ever
had to make. It broke me down to my knees,
led to my undoing,
utterly shattered the heart in me.
And now I am in the process
of becoming.

CHEERS

69

Our relationship was kismet—glorious beginning to disastrous end.

REVEALING REFLECTIONS

Wandering to the train tracks on crisp, fall days.
Each time a train would zip past imagining
all the ways life could quickly change.
Perhaps hitch a ride to a place to hide
in plain sight and quite a few detrimental things
I'd rather not say.

Rustling orange, yellow, red, brown leaves
made the most stunning scenery. Fallen tree logs
and cold cement blocks provided adequate seating
for a troubled mind to pass the time.
Each day sitting for hours figuring out what
I could offer this world, what it had for me.
Soon the days became shorter while
the air froze my chest. Which made it quite unbearable
sulking alone in the woods, lost in my head.

On the nights I couldn't sleep tossing and
turning in bed, even when the temperature dropped below,
I'd slide open the window and
lay listening instead. For in the woods
where I used to wander, trains would
honk their horns and zip by; perhaps
at another who would come to sit,
pass the time
and cry.

IN MOURNING

By the weeping willows,
sit down and wallow.
Our paths are never foreknown,
the ones we tread and follow.
Keep your treasured loves close as
there is no promise for tomorrow.
Then wash away your sorrows
since the time we have is borrowed.

LIMITED EDITION

72

The faults in our stars—a catastrophe, we were bound to fall apart.

I CAN'T STAND THE RAIN

Lucid dreams of faded faces,
what used to be trapped in altered places.
Dancing, romancing in a realm both near
and far. I know I'm sleeping, still,
here we are. What a strange feeling,
if I were awake, I'd be staring at the ceiling.
And when I do, I'll be right back to
the harsh realities of living with eyes wide open
when I'd rather be asleep dreaming,
with you.

SEARCH AND RESCUE

I've been searching for you
in the bodies of strangers,
hoping to feel your warmth again.

I've been listening to the breeze,
the whispering winds,
hoping to hear you speak again.

I've been sitting on that bench
amongst all the trees,
hoping to see you again.

Lastly, long lost love;
I've been tossing and turning
restless every night,
hoping to hold you—just
one more time.

STUNTED

75

Who knew I was the thorn in my side stunting my growth? Unfortunately, sometimes that's the way the story goes.

CHASING PAVEMENTS

Passers-by,
friendly,
you and I.
The first occurrence
so casually done,
continually 'til
two became one.
Spending time
intertwined;
knotted up,
our lives combined.
Eventually,
our lines crossed,
flags raised.
Energies all spent,
love now replaced.
What we've become,
you and I,
strangers lost in the world,
passing by.

WHAT LIES BENEATH

An ache deep within bones, crawling
under tiger-striped skin. Nestled to rest
in their first home; an experience passively mentioned,
with chances it might creep in.
Feeling overwhelmed, out of sorts—as
disconnected as an umbilical cord
clamped then snipped.

Not just a case of baby blues that'll pass
as the recovery months do. Come to terms with
lingering cruel pain and realize its name.
A roller-coaster ride of emotions with
unforeseeable moods; hopelessly waiting
for the motions to take a break, and
on the darkest days—contemplating
ways to escape. Struggling to enjoy
fleeting moments, their gentleness in a
realm of calm, so torturous as the days go on.

These after-effects from carrying
then birthing precious, innocent kin
are hard to fix with walks in the park
amongst trees, changing topics or
catching up on long-lost sleep.
Not a cut and paste solution after
falling in a black hole, or you're close to drowning;
wavering in the fourth trimester,
suffering from depression, post-partum.

IN MY SOLITUDE

There are times I wish if only to have:
more shoulders to rest my weary head,
more hands to hold when times are hard,
more lives to entrust my own.
Even for just one true friend to know me
better than I know myself. To trust me
as much as I trust them.

Because although I've become accustomed after all
these years, it's become quite too lonely
in my solitude.

STRANGERS WITH CANDY

Vividly bursting through my sensory system
with synapses flaring out of control. I was
feeling all shades of blue, then in popped
a multicolored dose of you.
Anticipating relief while awaiting the
desired release. One hit today, another
one tomorrow—*swallow this whole*
to combat your sorrows. Taking over
all five senses and impairing me with
this chemically imbalanced grief.
Feeling an urgency after each gulp to
escape my new distorted reality. Such despair
could not last the time prescribed, unfortunately.
Because with each consumption of you,
bits and pieces were getting lost that I forgot
I enjoyed having inside of me.

COMPANY'S CALLING

Have you ever wondered
how does their loneliness feel?
Is it loud and all-consuming
or does it whisper in the dark?
Like yours, does it pull at
them in all directions
and nit-pick at their souls?

PSYCHIC CONNECTION

81

We were finally together again, last night.
It seems though we're trapped,
only meeting in the in-between.
Vibrant memories and wishful realities.
Parts of our lives now stuck in a dream.

There have been nights I keep myself awake,
because seeing you warms my soul
and into pieces my heart breaks.
For certain the sun will rise way before noon.
I desperately hope you'll gaze upon it soon.

PANDORA'S BOX

82

Some people make a box and store it
up high on the shelf. Maybe for comfort
on a rainy day. Perhaps hoping for the one
they lost to return so they can weather
new storms together. Remembering the old days
made not of fulfilling content, but distorted bliss.
Walking by crowded closets envisioning
sunshine and happiness.

Was it a learned behavior or a mad idea?
To rip up love-filled pictures and
burn heartfelt letters. Throwing out jewelry
and trashing haunted clothes.
Who planted the seed that getting rid of
old lovers' treasures would also take the memories?
Because what's etched in my brain
passionately remains.

HIS NAME IS RALPH

Things to do with a broken-pain-pierced heart, a muddled-foggy-head, and a back-bending-cramping-nauseating stomach-ache:

- Climb out of bed when the children wake at six in the morning. No matter how late you fell asleep. It could've been half-past three or quarter to five. Quick now, on your feet.

- Tell them to turn the television down from blaring loudness to a quiet tone. Too low for the kids to hear their show, still too loud to mentally prepare yourself for the day.

- Put breakfast together or think of what they will eat. Different palettes, different faves—makes life interesting indeed.

- Shuffle around the messes here and over there. To-be folded clothes hanging off the couch and dining table. Food particles, dust, and treat wrappers in that corner. Dishes from the last few days piled with take-out garbage all over the counter. Mastering organizational skills with your patience challenging you to the test. Hey, you're trying your best.

- Make a list of all to get done by the evening: online learning, hunger curbing, bathroom cleaning, staring at the ceiling. If it's not one, it's the other. It's all such a bother; by the evening, everyone will be asleep dreaming.

- Eventually, there's some quiet, stillness in the air. It was possible to partially get through the list—doing any and everything to make the overbearing emotions feel calm. Take a load off now, sit on the comfy couch. Enjoy the muted chaos quickly before you get side-tracked again. In and out, breathe deep, please.

You'll have to finish your tasks another time—that elephant's coming back this way. It's astonishingly hard to take deep breathes when you feel as if your chest is being fucking compressed. Crushed and bruised with still so much to do. Toodles for now, we'll talk soon.

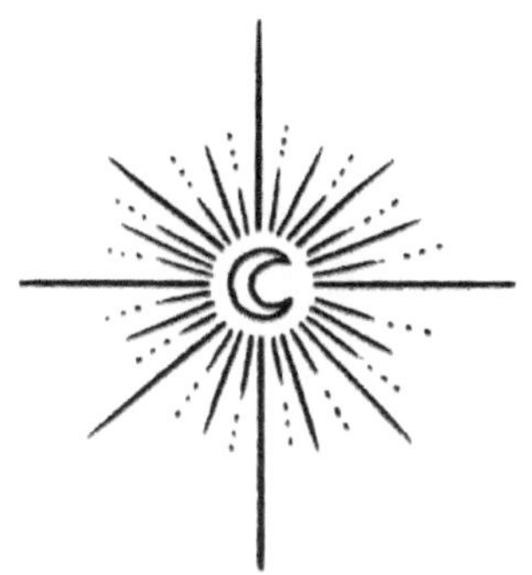

III.

Full Moon

on growth

HEARD IT THROUGH THE GRAPEVINE

Through the wire, I heard em say
—don't resolve affairs of the heart
in the absence of day. Trust not
the radiance as a guide through the smoke.
Wake up in the morning and process the facts
of all you need to know.
It's the sun you need
to see everything crystal clear.

But it just so happens that
in the night when my part of the world
has turned out the lights and
cozied up tight, all my words are in a hurry.
I'm too busy weighing my options
and sifting through my thoughts
to listen to what they might've said.

I'm listening to my heart
inside my wandering head
under the light of the moon,
a most understanding friend.

INTROSPECTION

88

Unearthing faded memories
once undeserving of attention.
Staring down the barrel of your soul.
A much-needed self-reflection.

STANDSTILL

89

It'll enter your life at a time so divine—everything you wished for unconsciously or once upon a time. An anchor stopping you dead in your tracks—a wrench in the wheels, putting all your plans on hold.

BE

On life's merry-go-round, one
experiences a flurry of things that'll lead
to smiles and frowns. Obstacles and triumphs
are never-ending as the end draws near.
So much advice given to those who'll
lend an ear. One of the simplest ways to comprehend
it all is to go through the motions and feel every pang.
Digest and embrace them,
just let them sit with you. Allow the feelings
to flow. When the lessons learned—not
when you think you're ready,
is when the ability comes
to release and let go.

TECTONIC SHIFT

91

I can feel a shift happening
beneath my feet.
I can feel it—deep inside.
When I am one with the stillness
and one with my breath.
Vibrating higher and
ready to accept Light power.

NOW

92

So, do it,
take the plunge.
You'll never know
what's on the other side,
unless you actually
start to try.
So, do it.

SOARING TO THE UNKNOWN

93

Where the sky meets the moon
and land is out of reach.
The destination of my dreams,
where all my fears remain unseen.

HEAR, HEAR!

Here's to the dark days.
Ones belonging to our shadows now
as we step into the Light
and abandon our old, wicked phase.

Now some claps to the good life.
We made this something out
of nothing but the scraps left
behind after countless heartbreaks.

Cheers to the lost times.
Hours spent imagining all the ways
our lives will change before it's over,
and we flat line.

SQUIGGLY LINES

95

Although I'm looking in, I don't feel as if I'm missing out. Life ebbs and flows as our emotions and energies do. I can settle, hope, and wish, but life will take me where I *need* to go.

MIRROR, MIRROR

In a puddle on the floor at the sight of stretches
and marks I struggle to adore. After dissecting
my being and unraveling frayed seams, I must
recall my sanity and settle my unnerved mind
as I am one-of-a-kind.
There is no place like home.
Stepping outside the confined mirror frame,
I am astounded by all this inherent body provides.
For one, strong legs to transport my
wandering spirit within. My body is a temple, and
secured inside is intelligence and wits,
glory and strength that won't be replicated or defied.
There is so much to say about why my figure is a gift.
I can't picture myself as another—I am
undoubtedly like any other.

I TURN TO YOU

97

Resilient through life's storms,
you are a beacon of light.
Unwavering against the
tests of time.

CONNECT THE DOTS

Divine intervention led to this immaculate creation,
an existence worth more than diamond rings.
Connect tiny freckles and marks of perfections
spread out across a canvas of supple skin.
Each dot marks the spot for the myriad of things
that make me who I am; family, friends,
unforgettable others—obstacles and fears
that shaped and broke me while on this journey.

Decisions made in haste and regrets to be faced.
Beauty-spots for where I was born and
every place I've laid my head since.
Speckles for dreams of traveling from sea to sea,
sprinkle them about the flesh for all the
experiences still to see. Imprints left from
lovers made under covers and rippled lines
each time patience stretched me thin.

Chips in the armour for aches I've embraced, and
times I had fallen and felt that in life,
I lost my place. Marked upon my grace is a mosaic
of influences that diluted my innocence: music for all
emotions, in theatres affirming devotions,
situations and people I had no business meeting.
Afterglows left always and forever etched in my being.
Firsts and lasts accumulated on this destined voyage
stippled and wrinkled on me—touches,
glances, hearty belly laughs;
countless moments that happen in a flash.

Standing firm as the earth spins, with a
constellation of starry perfections dispersed
upon a canvas of supple skin.
Connecting the dots each time my heart
grieves or sings, I'm embracing the multitude
of effects that make me who I am.

SHOTS

Speak and release,
the words need to flow.
With a pen in hand
or through the microphone.
Perhaps a few peers
you can confide in;
don't be worried about
your pride, friend.
Just, let it all go.

WATCH ME WHILE I BLOOM

Coursing through my lungs, synchronously, the fresh spring air envelops my skin. The sun is kissing my head as I dispel winter blues, embracing life's changes by shedding expired layers. Absorbing re-energizing sunlight, I begin a new and improved cycle of blossoming—within.

HER

102

There was you, now here's me—so much
space in between. If given the chance to sift through
times' sands, I'd be there to hold you tight.
Wipe streams of tears off your innocent face,
and squeeze those dainty little hands.
Through your dark, I'd beam bright—stay strong
right by your side.

AND THE MOON

Basking in the radiance
under the waning crescent of the moon.
Until waves of darkness
smash down serenity's walls,
drowning out built-up self-esteem.
Tides come crashing in
hurriedly releasing old fears of doom.

Although it's hard to see,
the new moon is here;
along with aches of bittered introspection,
a time for powerful new moon manifesting.
Realigning, deep diving to
unlock unconscious beliefs.
Divine intuition, a strong spiritual connection
bursting out, so, take heed.

Optimism stands firm for balancing throughout
this lunar cycle's cleansing energy.
A few nights still 'til
waxing crescent's shadow completely peels.
Prepare for clarity and contentment
as the harvest moon reveals.
Delight in the quintessence
of a recharged,
beaming moon.

LAZY SUNDAY FAVORITES

104

I broke myself into pieces to devoid
any semblance of you—pulled my insides
out to remove your echoes of doubt.
A stranger I became to the world and
everything I knew before, teetering
on the edge—needing to rearrange my unfit pieces
to form my grander puzzle.

SEEDS FOR SOWING

105

Here we grow again while
waiting for the fog to clear.
Intentions set, stars are aligning.
Don't get lost in soul-sucking despair.

YELLOW BRICK ROAD

Steady foot in front of the other,
these roads are always winding.
Change in theory is easy.
The journey will be the toughest.

BREAK THROUGH THE EARTH

With tresses all there, the strands each
hold a story: what I'm feeling that day,
the cost to style it. How much pride is beaming
when I wear a puff so freely,
throwing caution to the wind.

Magical gold and red strands that'd peek through
and glow in the sunlight. Passed down
by my father, DNA from the isles and hills.
Curls and coils mingling together, what a
beautiful sight. A gift from my mother, with
tales interwoven of ancestors stole,
dating decades back to the slave trade.

Regularly it seemed that wondrous crown
set boundaries, as if suffocating or
drowning me. It wasn't the weight or sight that
did the damage, but the restrictions I put
on myself—to speak. An internal struggle to release
the emotions, so burdening.

The splitting of dry ends, working up
the corkscrew and coiled shafts 'til
damage had to be clean cut off.
With all the volume my hair can speak,
it only made sense I needed to be without
to begin this journey. Getting to the root
of the problems and working out all my kinks.

My distinctive process as I begin psychological
metamorphosis. Releasing, redefining, realigning;
a dire need to transform anew,
embracing all of me—yet most importantly,
regaining peace deep within.

IN THE WILDERNESS

109

You must trek through the darkness to bathe in the light.

WAITING FOR MY ROCKET TO COME

The thrill of it, the chase.
So much pressure and
time I didn't want to waste.
I couldn't wait to grow up,
yet I can't believe I did.
Riding down a lane of memories into
a place called now.
Never did I imagine being
alive to see all this.

BARE

And so it went—peeling back the layers, day by day. Expired versions stripped; overexposed, right down to the core. Unrecognizable before stepping through the next chapter's door.

DEFROSTING

Today was a good day, I did all
the things I set out to do. Simply because
I wasn't disabled by feeling so blue.
These periods can last long when
all I want to be is still. Locked up
in my ice-cold castle feeling
empty on a hill.

I am the queen and, I am the guard
of walls so impenetrable it would break
your heart. On the wondrous days I let my
barrier down, I become one with the Light
and ascend above limits. Beyond my ice fortress
releasing the aching gloom.
And it's on those days that my late buds
prepare for bloom.

ONE

113

This smooth skin I'm in.
carrying case, house of love
soon will turn to dust.

TRAILBLAZING

You can go the distance,
you can play the part.
None of it will matter
without the fire in your heart.

LEAP OF FAITH

Remember when one of the scariest things was jumping off the jungle gym? Or out of trees? Remember that feeling of psyching yourself up to go? Feeling anxious and sweaty, getting in the position to make the jump. Counting down while closing your eyes to imagine what'll happen next. 5, 4, 3, 2 ....

Leap. Take the plunge. Say everything you've been dying to say. Put yourself out there. Go where you haven't gone before. If you fail, at least you can figure out what went wrong and try again. The biggest regret will be not trying at all.

Fight through the anxiety.

BRAINPOWER

At my core,
there's been purpose manifested.
Deep in my soul,
I feel spiritual alignment
transpiring.

PASSION PIT

Some words I put to feelings: a
reeling in my soul of emotions
I thought no longer dwelled inside. It
nit-picks at the anxiety I shoved
below the surface to hide.
The second I feel I've regained control,
I'm back to the ache—a reeling in my soul.

Some words I put to feelings: phrases,
praises, gestures said without a care.
Seeing straight through the smoke, right
to what's there. Hidden in plain sight, it
is a reeling in my soul
pulling me towards the Light.

To a promise made in darkness for
better days, happier tomorrows.
While yearning for clarity, peace, and joy;
these rewards are only attainable as
I work hard and go towards.

REVITALIZED

There is triumph in emerging from darkness,
rewards to be won.
When pulling yourself from
places of which you've told no one.

STEP ONE

I want to fill you with so much love
until it seems your seams will burst.
I want to place the world at your feet
and take away any chances for misery.
I want to be everything, no—I need to be
everything you'll need from me and more.
I need to become the best version of
myself though—first.

CHOSEN

Each moment with a loved one or unexpected encounter with a stranger is meant to be. The places your journey leads to and everything in between. What we experience throughout life teaches us and provides new opportunities as we navigate through the vast unknown.

BRICK BY BORING BRICK

A wolf in sheep's clothing, the bird,
and the prey. An angel searching for Light,
the boulder stuck in the way. Until the work
is complete, and all debts are paid,
enjoy the prison of your mind
amongst each brick you've laid.

KEEPSAKE

122

You glow different when you're living in your truth.

Embrace it.

ANDREW

123

A vision foretold my presence
and each blessing that's ever crossed my path
have been cosmic presents. Every single person,
trials and errors, happy moments and
those of despair or terror. All the knowledge I hope
to gain, millions of memories still to flood
my mind's frame. If I were gifted the chance
to live this life again, everything
would be the same.

WRITING THERAPY

124

Lines, verses,
handwritten, in cursive.
Words flow
then flee my mind.
Leaving space,
room for me to breathe.

NOSTALGIA, ULTRA

125

A sense of longing and belonging
of the known and unknown.
Places I've been and
ones I'll never see.
People I miss and
those I hope to meet.
Waiting for new beginnings
while dreading their ends.
Still, I'm excited for changes
to come, again and again.

IT WAS WRITTEN

When you are no longer your trauma,
where do you run? Who do you become
when you're no longer *that* one?
Through the Dark Night of the Soul,
a third-eye opening path one can go on
to awaken and become.
Grow into your destined role.

SIMMER DOWN

Still
There is magic there
Let it simmer, let
And look within and
Then in a moment it will change then
Wait a while
And be
Still

WANDERER

128

I feel alive in the Winter, the season of my birth.
Crisp air, dead leaves, chirp-less mornings,
empty trees. Everything I am, contrary to the life
I imagined to be alive to see. A new chapter
is beginning, my soul is feeling at ease.

IT'LL TEAR YOU UP

The trouble with love is all the places
it can hide. It'll have you searching in the
body of another and another, continuously
craving the perfect lover. The one to
set you straight, let you be free. Until
figuring out what wholly being loved means.
All the while, a strenuous quest or
so it seemed while lost in your head.

True love is waiting deep down inside.
Look in the mirror,
fall in love with the one in sight.

DENIAL TO REVIVAL

Searching, digging, hurting, and healing.
Sifting through old lies and buried
alibis. Covered up, under the layers where
worries used to drown. Drinking to feel happy,
drunk to dull pain. Fumble over words, come to
my senses as I'm stumbling in the rain.
From all the places Guardian Angels
saved me from, I'm lucky for every
given chance I received to carry on.

TRANSFORMATIVE PERIODS

Stolen from places of comfort,
keeping you hostage
to hold you accountable.
Only to be released when
you've surrendered to the
Will of the Universe.

MAGICAL CREATURES

Words get in the way,
they sift through all the aches.
Ones burrowed under layers
of bandages to mask the pain.

NATURE OF THINGS

133

Tend to a garden of your own and
you'll see what you've always known.
The weeds in life will come and go,
wherever beauty is grown.

SET FOR LIFE

134

Growing up, I wished for any name except
my own. Many times, I desperately longed for a
different body to call home. Twenty-nine trips
around the sun—what a battle it's been to settle in.
Here I am, I exist between the hairs on my head
and my red nail-polished toes.
Pouring my heart and soul out—in
poetry and prose.

THE DARKEST ROAD TRAVELED

Drift off to space or float out in the sea.
When I envisioned my future, this wasn't
it, unfortunately. I imagined a void—nothingness
and doom. A dimension that I'd enter and
plunge in the emptiness—forever.

Searching for comfort and love in others
before finding it within myself, before I genuinely
enjoyed existing. Years spent keeping the lid on
everything, barely able to find any solace within
which was needed before any healing could begin.

Lost at the bottom of bottles trying to suppress
everything—loneliness, rage, and pain, attainable
hopes, and dreams. Shapeshifting through my days
until stability was re-established
long enough for me to find the way.

Many moons, I feel I've finally found my footing.
Walking on this journey of enlightenment,
a path my soul desperately longed to see.
Releasing any pains that hindered me.
A realization after long-lost years is that
it wasn't my desire *to end*,
but my need **to be**.

FROM THE AUTHOR

A special acknowledgement to my family and friends, to anyone who's ever connected with me and my words—thank you for being apart of my journey.

The moon's phase changes throughout its cycle, as do we; loving, aching, growing, and more on this journey called Life.

Thank you so much for reading and supporting my

work!

AndreanaWarlow.ca

IG: AndreanaWrites

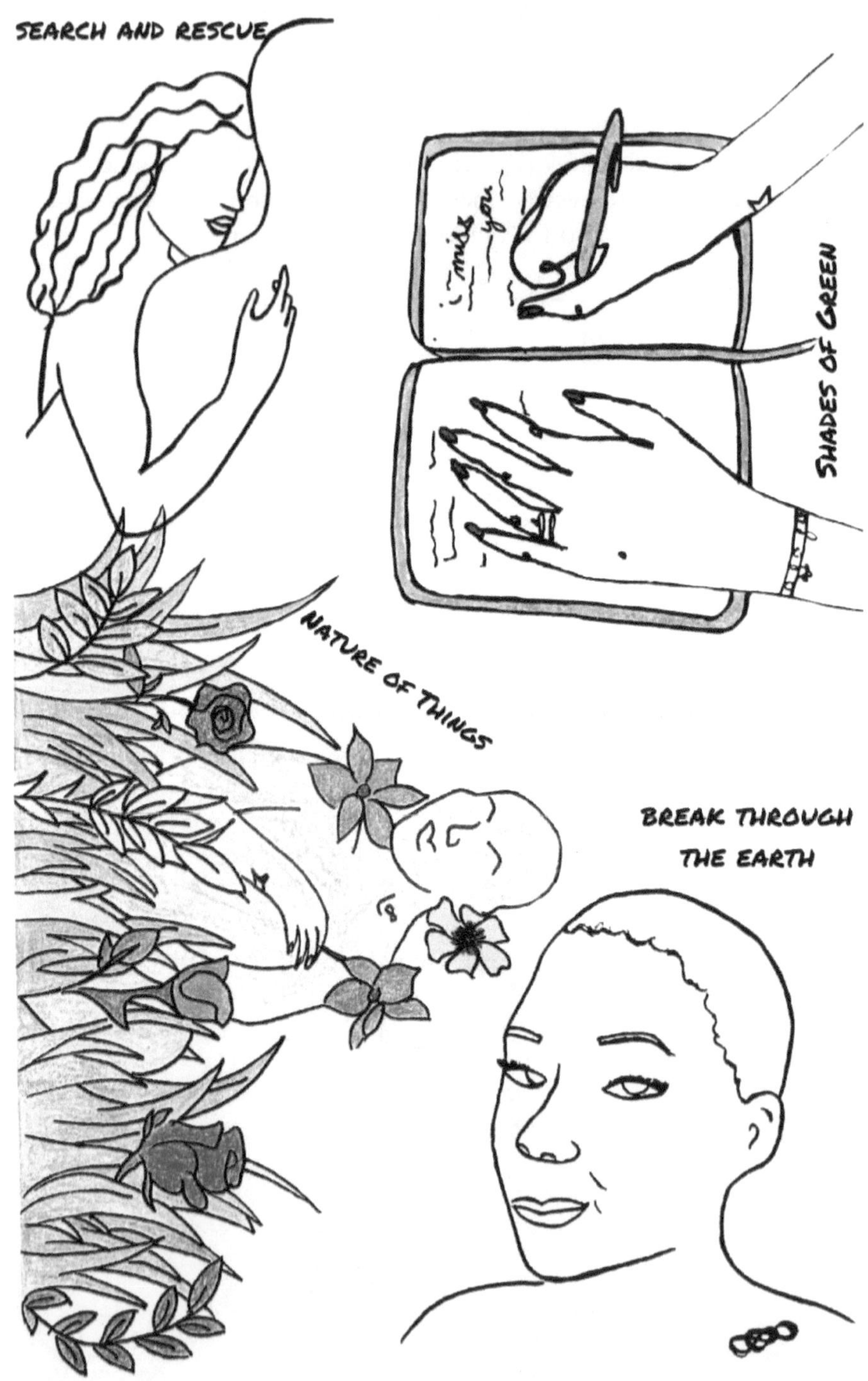
SEARCH AND RESCUE
i miss you
SHADES OF GREEN
NATURE OF THINGS
BREAK THROUGH
THE EARTH

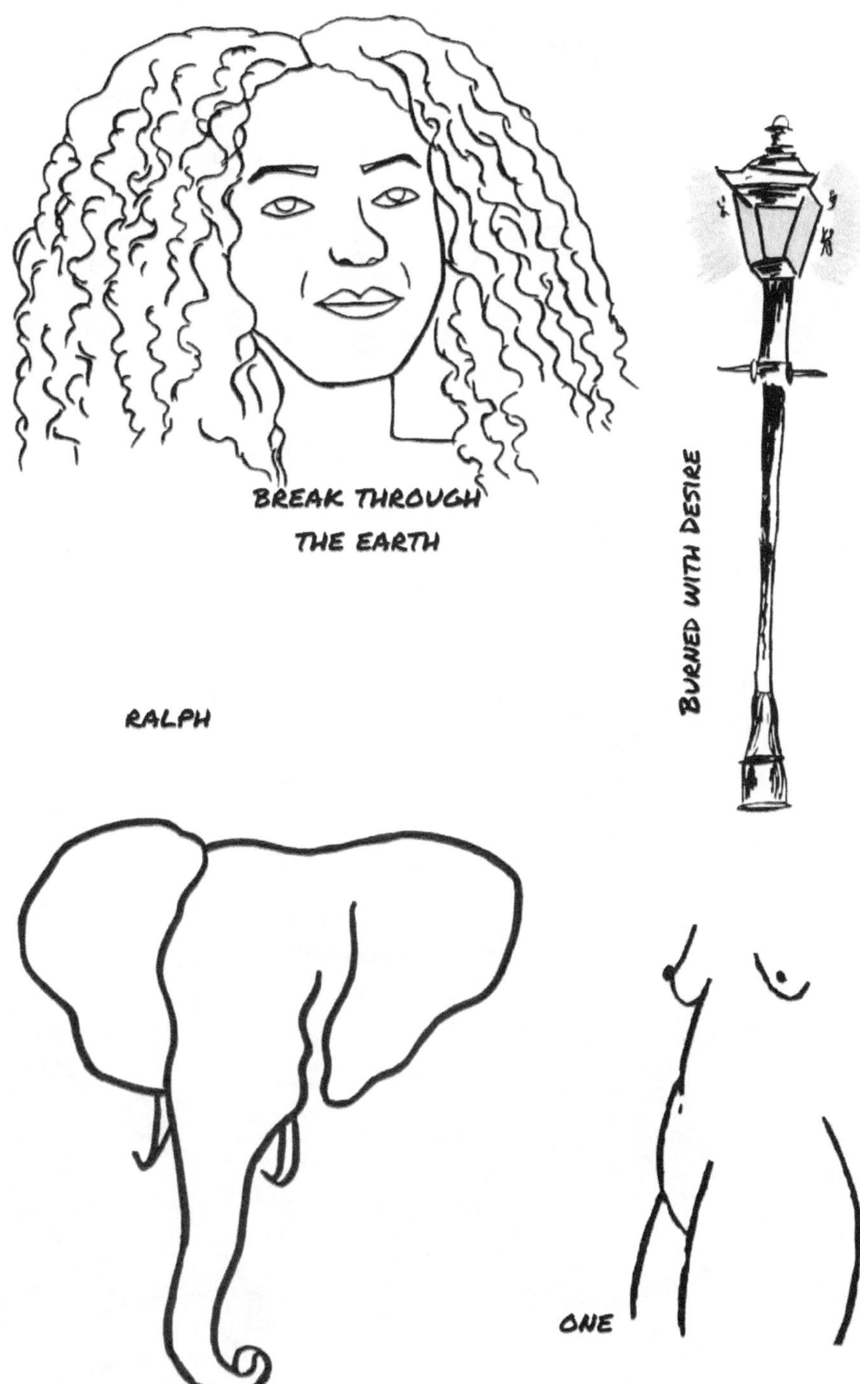
BREAK THROUGH
THE EARTH
RALPH
BURNED WITH DESIRE
ONE

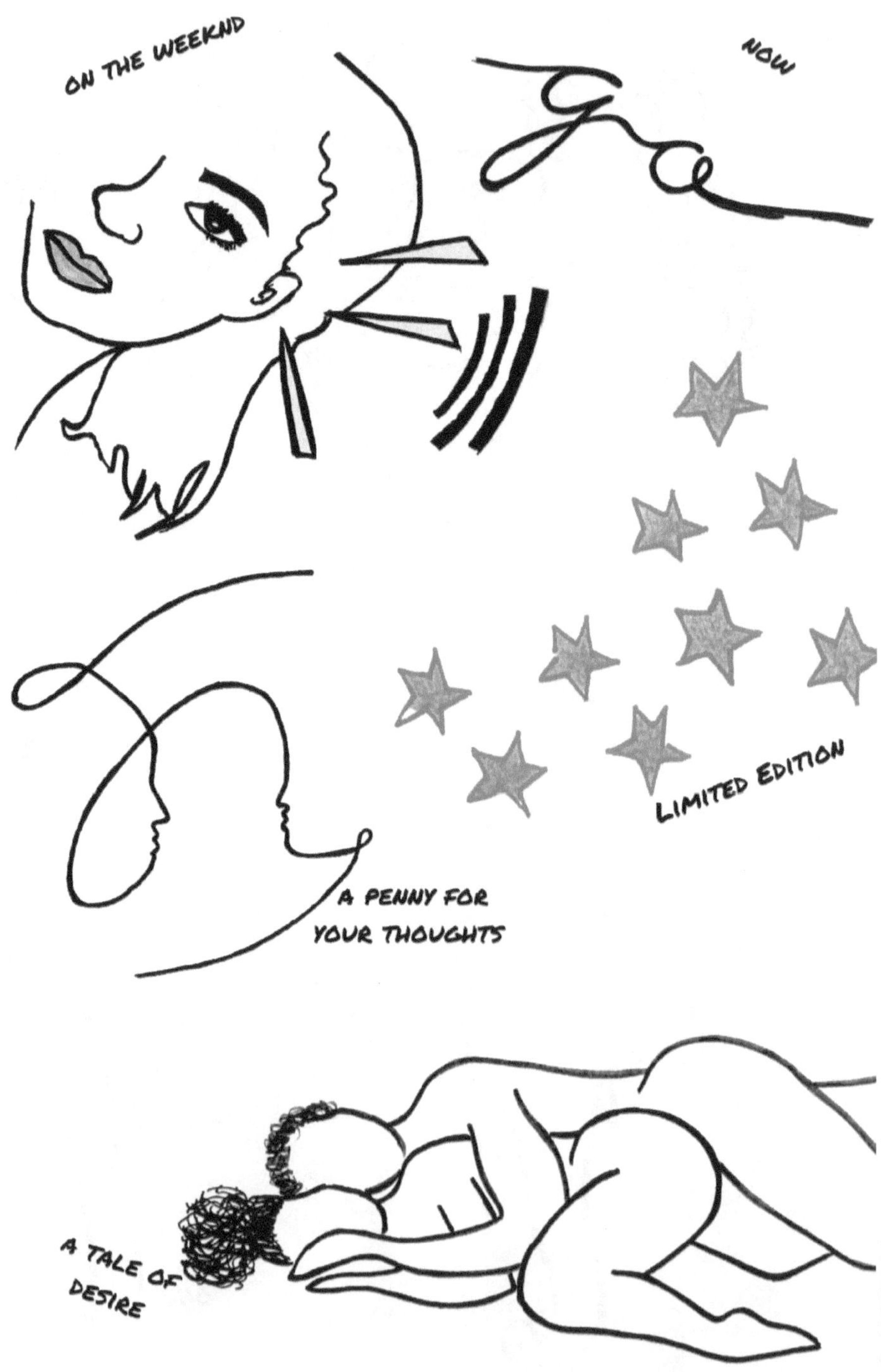
ON THE WEEKND
NOW
A PENNY FOR
YOUR THOUGHTS
LIMITED EDITION
A TALE OF DESIRE